NORTH NORFOLK

Images

Classic photographs from the Eastern Daily Press archives

Trevor Heaton

Eastern Daily Press

Acknowledgements

I am grateful to the following for their advice in my research: May Ayers, Richard Batson, Henry "Shrimp" Davies BEM, Martin Kirby, Eric Mason and Chris Stokes. My thanks, as ever, to Philip Preston and Peter Waters for their help and enthusiasm, and to the dedication and professionalism of the Norwich reprographic team: Richard Bunting, David Cartledge, Patrick Frary, Stephen Godfrey, John Hutchinson, Steven Jennings, Sue Morse, Steven Riseborough and Martin Rodwell.

ISBN 0-9502952-7-2

Front cover: Blakeney Quay, pictured in July 1970
Back cover: Happisburgh Lighthouse, September 1971

An Eastern Daily Press Classics production

This book is dedicated to Katie and Becky Heaton

Contents

Introduction

In his book on the county published in 1890, William Dutt gave this simple summing-up of the character of North Norfolk: "It is all so enchanting."

And that, in a nutshell, is the essence of the charm of this beautiful part of East Anglia.

This book has taken some of the best pictures from the matchless local archives of the Eastern Daily Press to present a portrait of this unique part of England and its people. The photographs mainly cover the period of the Fifties, Sixties and early Seventies.

So where exactly is 'North Norfolk'? Descriptions vary, from the area defined by the local authority of that name, to any part of the north-facing Norfolk coast. For some, North Norfolk is Cromer, Sheringham and Poppyland. For my part, I have taken the area as being that bordered by Wells, just south of Fakenham and then straight across the county to include Aylsham, North Walsham and Happisburgh.

And what a beautiful slice of the county it is. The landscape is mainly of gently rolling hills increasing in size until they become the famous Cromer-Holt Ridge and the dramatic, though fragile, cliffs of the north-east corner of the county. The rural way of life, although not as labour- and horse-intensive as in previous generations, remains a key factor in local life.

The sea has been a constant backdrop to the story of North Norfolk since the last Ice Age and its influence continues to exert a huge influence on local life. It has, after all, enabled the development of popular holiday resorts and a fishing industry. And then there is its darker side – floods, ships forced aground or worse, and the conditions that have kept the area's lifeboatmen busy over the years.

This book includes many pictures of those who play by it, work in it, live by it – and sometimes regret its presence.

I have chosen photographs of the ordinary people of North Norfolk at work and at play, from the farmer harrowing his field in a chill February drizzle to the holidaymaker and his family stretching out at Wells beach in the warm August sunshine, from a reluctant donkey at a children's Nativity to villagers enjoying a summer fun-fair.

Sometimes the pictures record the passing of a way of life – some of the deserted railway stations awaiting the Beeching axe are particularly poignant – yet others record the apparently changeless nature of many beautiful North Norfolk landscapes.

But, of course, there have been changes and this book includes pictures of developments such as the natural gas terminal at Bacton, a major landmark in the ancient story of Norfolk.

That said, it is a proud boast of North Norfolk that its rural charm is only a stone's throw away from even the busiest road. Take a turn off the A148 or A149 and within a few miles you will find yourself in a maze of country lanes where the heady scent of elderflower and the churr-churr call of a startled pheasant can be found cheek-by-jowl with beautiful medieval churches and flint-cobbled cottages.

In his book Dutt added "You are indeed in the beauty spot of Norfolk, and it is difficult to tell a tithe of its charms."

Thankfully, even in the hurly-burly of the closing years of the century, that remains as true as ever – and long may it remain so.

Trevor Heaton

Chapter One

Countryside Charms

A precarious perch for the EDP photographer on the roof of Paston Tithe Barn in this view, taken on April 20th 1953. Workmen from Messrs R W Farman of North Walsham were working on the 155ft-long 16th-century barn.

A hand-painted sign on the rickety fence advertises "Evensong Sunday 3pm" in this charming composition of Bessingham Church taken on October 24th 1948.

The rural quiet of North Norfolk is superbly captured in this splendid July 1958 Ingworth scene.

Children admire the new village sign at Blakeney, with its appropriate nautical centrepiece. The sign was presented to the village by the local branch of the WI and unveiled by Lady Margaret Barry on June 23rd 1966.

They wouldn't attract a second glance nowadays, but the march of technology to the most rural of North Norfolk villages led the EDP photographer who took this previously unpublished picture of Wighton in 1962 to write a note to his picture editor: "Sorry about the post and overhead wires. I have never seen a village with so many... they are everywhere."

Homeward-bound: The pale sunshine of a January 1950 afternoon lights up Cley village church and the farmworker taking his horse and tumbril home.

Storm clouds gather in this 1956 view of All Saints' Church at Morston.

(Above) The timeless beauty of Salthouse marshes, pictured in late November 1966.

(Right) A scene of rural calm in this July 1967 view of Weybourne.

This pretty winter view of Paston Mill was taken on February 4th 1963. But most people were too busy trying to keep warm to admire the picture postcard views across the county. The EDP reported "No let up in worst blizzard since 1947" on its front page, and local people were dealing with temperatures such as the minus 9 degrees C (16 degrees F) on the night this picture was taken. An indication of just how cold things were was provided in the same day's EDP when it carried a picture of a snow plough in action – on Diss Mere!

The closure of Trunch brewery in the early 1950s marked the end of an era not just for the village, but for Norfolk too. For the Trunch operation was thought to be the last of the old-style village breweries to close in the county. Brewing on the site began in 1803, taking advantage of an excellent water supply. William Primrose built the brewery in 1857, but the development came at a time when better communications and the growth of "tied" public houses were causing a concentration of production in fewer, large-scale breweries. In 1852 there were 88 "common breweries" – ie for the local trade – but by 1900 this had shrunk to 25. At the time of its take-over by Morgans in 1952, Trunch brewery had nine Houses, including the Crosskeys Hotel, North Walsham, Bath Hotel Cromer, Red Lion Hotel, Aylsham, Anchor Inn, Blakeney and the Barge Inn at Antingham.

Don't look down... thatchers Mr J Sturman and Mr A Carman pause for a picture while working on the roof of Overstrand Cricket Club's pavilion on May 6th 1955.

(Overleaf) An early 1950s view of the River Glaven at Glandford. Across the river the parish church of St Martin dominates the skyline.

The flint tower of Wighton parish church had resisted hundreds of years of the worst that the weather could throw at it. But then one November day in 1965 there came one gale too many. Tons of masonry crashed into the churchyard and smashed into a road. Thanks to the generosity of Canadian businessman Leeds Richardson – whose family originated from Wighton – the tower was rebuilt in 1976. The March 1977 picture (below) shows the new flintwork weathering in nicely.

Chapter Two

Oh, Dr Beeching!...

Members of the Norfolk Railways Society enjoyed a special day at Mundesley on May 15th 1960. They are pictured round a J15 steam engine and are being given an instructional talk by British Railways driver Mr G A Betts. They later started out on a trip between Mundesley and North Walsham. The society had hired this section of the line for the afternoon and each member took his turn at the controls.

The time-honoured safety procedure of exchanging "tablets" on a single track line to ensure one train only is on it was performed for the last time on the Melton Constable-Sheringham line on April 4th 1964. The driver of the last passenger train, Ernest Stapelton (right) left Holt for the journey to Sheringham accompanied by the sound of line detonators.

When news of the Beeching axe for the Mundesley-North Walsham line was announced in March 1963 – when the EDP took this picture – it did not come as any great surprise. Almost exactly a decade earlier the link to Cromer had been closed, so in a sense the station, which was built in 1898, had been living on borrowed time. Nevertheless, local people pointed out that a 45-minute train journey to Norwich compared very favourably with the 80-minute crawl by bus. But soon the 14 trains which travelled each way daily were just a memory.

Eve of destruction: Holt station in March 1963. The line between Holt, Weybourne, Sheringham and Cromer was opened on June 16th 1887, later being amalgamated with other railways in East Anglia to form the grandly-named Midland and Great Northern railway – known in rather more down-to-earth terms by local people as the "Muddle and Get Nowhere". But under-investment, and social and transport changes meant the rapid demise of branch lines after British Railways was nationalised in 1948. The Melton Constable-Cromer section survived until 1964 – but the writing was on the wall, apparently, much earlier: the Eastern Daily Press told in 1962 how a Holt woman tried to buy a ticket to the town from a Yorkshire station, only for the ticket clerk to find that BR had literally crossed the station off its network map. Although the Holt station site is now covered by the town's bypass, the North Norfolk Railway has re-opened a station on its outskirts at High Kelling.

A slice of railway nostalgia – and a large dollop of poetic licence from the photographer. Alec Tuck was pictured apparently putting his back into operating the former Wells station turntable in the mid-1950s. But things are not quite what they seem in this evocative photo. His brother John later pointed out that the shot was clearly posed as the engine had already been turned, ready to roll backwards to the engine shed. Another give-away for those in the know was the image of the engine driver, Bill Chapman, with his back to camera looking rather less than concerned while his fireman did the work. John noted: "Mr Chapman would have had his ears badly bent should he have left his fireman to push the engine round on his own. Men have been ruptured for less." Alec, who has since died, was a member of a true railway family. His father, Ted, was the last driver in charge of the Wells loco department, while brother John was a railway clerk and another brother, Geoffrey, also worked as a fireman.

The first arrivals at the old Sheringham Station following its closure as a
British Rail site roll into view. The Midland and Great Northern Joint Railway
Society brought the engines to the station on June 5th 1967, one of the first
landmarks which led to the eventual founding of the much-loved Poppy Line.
Among the arrivals were engines from 1912 and 1932, five coaches and two
diesel rail buses.

Melton Constable was the Crewe Junction of North Norfolk... until Beeching. By 1969 – when this picture was taken – this once well-kept railway platform was a sad wilderness of weeds and boarded-up windows. When the station was eventually pulled down two years later to make way for an automatic telephone exchange, one of the intriguing items found was a 1911 circular giving directions to railwaymen on how to cope with the national seamen's strike.

This is the scene at the former North Walsham Town Station just five short years after the end of the M and GN. Already the trackbed has become overgrown. In the distance the sweep of the Norwich-Sheringham line can just be seen – complete with diesel railcar. The picture was taken in August 1964.

Heave!: March 15th 1975 saw volunteers from the Poppy Line work through the night
This enabled the delivery of two Pullman cars from the famous Brighton Belle line

to make ready a length of track from the new BR Sheringham station to the old site.
to the North Norfolk Railway.

An undated
aerial view of
Sheringham,
probably
from the
1950s.

Chapter Three

View From The Top

One of the earliest pictures in our collection, this view of Cromer was taken from left to right, with the Royal Links Hotel dominating the skyline.

the Cromer–Norwich train on September 3rd 1948. Mill Road sweeps round from

November 1966 saw an historic announcement for North Norfolk. Shell and the Gas Council announced their chosen site to build a natural gas terminal was to be at Bacton. The announcement was greeted with disbelief; the EDP reported "the first reaction locally was of undiluted hostility" A spokesman for Shell promised "no smells and very little interference" from the 100-acre development. This picture was taken on November 4th, as the controversy gathered pace. The planned site was next to the Mundesley Holiday Camp (centre).

Sealing the joints of Cley's famous mill in May 1967.

(Overleaf) The Stead and Simpson store is the focal point of this marvellous view of Cromer taken from the church tower on June 20th 1964.

We're not sure of the date of this view of West Runton, save that it was probably taken in the 1980s. The church lies at the heart of this popular holiday village, with the ranks of caravans seemingly – thanks to the trick of perspective – only yards from the crashing North Sea waves.

(Previous page) The unmistakable form of Cromer pier dominates this fascinating July 1976 aerial view of the town.

Two horses make their way across a street in Trunch in September 1950, in a picture taken from the top of the church tower.

(Overleaf) A 1970 aerial view of Wells, with the maze of fisherman's yards and streets near the quayside contrasting with the more spacious modern development elsewhere in the town. Over on the right hand side a further reminder of changing times as an industrial estate takes shape by the old railway site.

Although Fakenham has seen much development in recent years, the swift transformation from town to country south of the river Wensum is still, thankfully, largely unchanged from this spectacular viewpoint, at the top of its 115ft church tower. This picture dates from September 12th 1959.

Chapter Four

We Plough The Fields...

The chill in the
February rain is
almost tangible
as Gipsy and Mr
F Lincoln carry
out harrowing at
Biswell Farm,
Sidestrand, in
1961.

A traditional scene of threshing and baling at Capt D Keith's Sculthorpe Lodge Farm on September 6th 1966. The corn has been carted from the field where the feeder puts the crop into the thresher.

Mr A Robotham, left, and Jack Mullinger, with Molly, stop for a mardle on November 4th 1967 while unloading mangolds on John Ashworth's Lodge Farm at Stibbard.

Where there's muck... there's even more muck. Workers at Mr Thistleton-Smith's farm at Pudding Norton use their "muck cromes" to rake out piles of good old-fashioned manure ready for spreading with a four-tine fork. A Ferguson tractor on the right of the picture is a reminder of the onset of modern machinery in this September 1957 picture.

In its time, Hempton Sheep Fair was one of the biggest sheep fairs in Norfolk, with up to 12,000 animals sold. But it was already in decline when the picture (above) was taken on September 1st 1954. By 1969 auctioneer Colin Beck (right) was being pictured knocking down the final lots of the final fair. When Lot 78 was sold to Harry Hammond of Beetley at 1.40pm on September 3rd 1969 it was the end of an era for the whole of Norfolk, as Hempton had been the very last traditional sheep fair in the county.

Teamwork: The unmistakable North Norfolk landmark of 'Beeston Bump' is clearly visible in this evocative March 1956 study of Mr R Mallett with his team of Jolly and Jack chain harrowing at Beeston Regis.

An elevator and tractor give a boost to old-fashioned muscle-power in this July 3rd 1954 picture of haymaking at Great Farm, Saxthorpe.

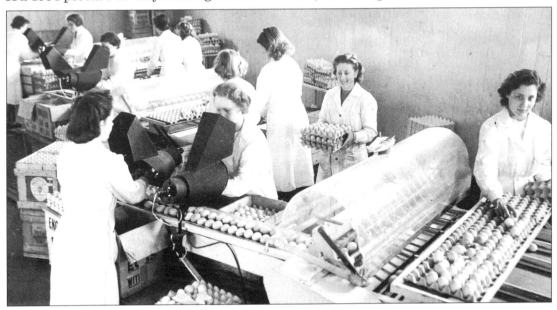

North Walsham Egg Packing Station had just moved to its Furze Hill premises when this picture was taken on May 20th 1953. A staff of 18 candled and graded 432,000 eggs a week, collected from 1300 to 1400 local farmers and small-scale producers. Most were for the Norfolk market, with the surplus sent to London.

Chapter Five

The Restless Sea

What a whopper: John Lee with the enormous nine-pound crab which he and his father-in-law, Coxswain Henry Davies, of Cromer No 1 lifeboat, hauled up in September 1958. The crab, the claws of which measured more than 16 inches, was too big even for the crab pot – it was found clinging to the side.

That's swell... the Sheringham lifeboat "Foresters Centenary" is launched into heavy seas in August 1951 to mark Lifeboat Day.

For those in peril: Sheringham Lifeboat Service, August 12th 1967.

Proud moment: George Culley of East Runton – pictured standing by the sternpost – was clearly delighted with his new boat Nigella (Love-in-a-Mist) which he had just sailed round from Great Yarmouth on September 2nd 1959. The Nigella, 20 ft long with an 8ft beam, was one of the fastest North Norfolk crab boats with a speed of more than eight knots. It was built at Mr W May's Potter Heigham yard, which had also produced a boat for Cromer fisherman Dennis Gaff. That summer was one of the warmest since the war and some of the many visitors to the coast that year can be seen in the background.

"Yew got a bit of water in thare, ol' pardner..." or that's what the onlookers seem to be saying as they watch the job of baling out tidewater under way. This storehouse on West End at Wells quayside was one of those affected on September 29th 1969 by the worst pounding the town had seen since 1953. The surge also carried away no fewer than 40 beach huts.

When it comes to talk of flooding, of course, the inundation of January 1953 remains notorious. Pictured is a dramatic aerial view of the floods at Cley. The famous windmill can be seen on the left of the picture.

The long, back-breaking work of filling in one of the many breaches caused was under way in this March 19th 1953 view at Wells.

(Overleaf) The floods had begun to recede by the time this picture was taken of Salthouse. The damage left by the surge is clearly to be seen. The photographer described it as "reminiscent of wartime devastation" and it is hard to disagree with his verdict. The suffering of some of the people of Salthouse went on much longer – seven of them, including three elderly couples, had to wait until November 1954 before the Lord Mayor's Flood Distress Fund would give them help, their cause being championed by councillor Joan Watson Cook.

The January 1978 floods which hit the East coast were the worst since 1953, with extensive damage as far inland as Wisbech. At Wells the power of the waves was graphically illustrated by the ships and boats washed up on the quay – along with tons of silt and seaweed. The EDP carried pictures of the stranded vessels with the simple heading "Parked at Wells". It was not until almost two weeks later that the biggest of the "parked" ships was returned to the water. This was the 125-ton dead-weight Function, which had just unloaded its cargo of cereal pellets when the waves struck. Putting it back in the water (pictured right) involved a considerable feat of logistics and a £1.25 million crane. Hundreds of spectators braved the January chill to watch her return to the harbour – but not until a bottle of champagne had been cracked across her (thankfully undamaged) bows.

Making a splash: A spectacular shot of Cromer No 1 lifeboat being launched for Life

boat Day on August 7th 1958.

Well, that's one way to get to the shops: Cyrilo Butler, Commodore of Blakeney Sailing Club, goes out for a spin in his Javelin class dinghy up Westgate Street to the foot of High Street. Mr Butler, of Manor House, Cley, made the unusual trip to win a wager that he would not be able to sail up the street on the predicted 31.2ft tide. He did, with more than two feet depth to spare, thanks to the highest predicted tide for three centuries.

No, not snow –but foam. Tons of it were whipped up by 40mph winds on June 29th 1960, baffling local people from Cromer to Sheringham and beyond. Cromer's east beach was particularly badly affected, with drifts up to three feet deep. Local people swore the phenomenon was unprecedented, but council officials said it had happened before – and rejected suggestions the effect was caused by the build-up of detergents in outfall water. The phenomenon – put down to algae – has happened several times.

This splendid – and historic – picture, taken in June 1966, celebrates surviving crew members of the famous Sheringham lifeboat, the Henry Ramey Upcher. Pictured are, from left, Teddy (Fiddy) West, aged 72; Bob (Joyful) West, 68; Jimmy (Paris) West, 70; Walter (Pongo) Little, 74; Henry (Pinny) Little, 73, and Bob (Rally) West. Seated is Henry (Joyful) West, aged 80. The lifeboat was launched on October 21st 1894 and rescued 202 people between 1894 and 1935. It had been put on display in 1965, after a campaign by local woman Mrs Lizzie Mason. The reporter wrote of the now-retired boat: "Now the dramas of her brave life are over. Now she rests peacefully in retirement, her bows facing the sea where once she defied the waves as her crew strained with courage and fortitude at the oars."

The Dutch vessel Jonet ran aground at Mundesley in March 1969. Refloating it proved an impossible task, and after a week efforts were abandoned and its cargo of fertiliser sold off. The ship was later dismantled for scrap. Our picture, taken on March 15th, shows members of Mundesley Coastguard Rescue Equipment Company in action, under the leadership of auxiliary coastguard Denis Nearney. They fired a rocket to try to get a line aboard, but the cable later snapped.

The homecoming: John Lee (left) and Arthur Harrison pack the biggest crab catch of the season, on May 1st 1951. Next to Mr Harrison is Ted Cook, a local character who used to help the town's fishermen unload their catch.

Cromer fishermen Dick Davies and Peter Mayes hoist bags of steaming hot whelks, destined for the London market, from boiling coppers on November 23rd 1954. The fishermen had returned with the shellfish from a six-hour trip to the Bacton grounds. The average catch of whelks was around 13 skeps (bushels) for which the fishermen received around 9s (45p) each skep. But the whelking – described as a "filling-in activity" – was never very popular with the fishermen of the time as prices were low and the chances high of losing valuable pots to late-season bad weather.

April 1951, and Cromer fishermen attend to their boats, including the Peggy (owned by George "Crow" Rook), Boy Leslie (Leslie Harrison jnr), Lewis James (Lewis Harrison), Silver Spray (Jack Davies) and Boy Jimmy. The last-named was involved in one of the most moving tragedies in Cromer's recent history when in June 1953 it was swamped just 150 yards off shore, claiming the lives of Ted Bussey and brothers Jimmy and Frank Davies. Veteran lifeboatman Henry Blogg collapsed as he tried to launch a rescue boat, and Frederick Wells, son of a Cromer greengrocer, plunged fully-clothed into the sea in a desperate attempt to reach the three. The accident stunned the town, and the poignant reports in the EDP of the aftermath still make for moving reading. More than 1700 people packed every nook and cranny in the parish church for their funeral, with another 1000 lining the streets in silent tribute. Coroner L H Allwood spoke for the whole of Norfolk when he said: "It is a dreadful thing that this accident has taken away these three fine men."

(Overleaf) Two Overstrand villagers stand mardling, apparently totally unconcerned by the spectacular sea pounding the shore behind them. The photograph was taken on September 29th 1969.

There was a rather large bunker at the 17th at the Royal Cromer Golf Club on May 17th 1962, thanks to a cliff fall of thousands of tons of sand and soil. The fall, which followed another just three weeks earlier, is typical of the seemingly relentless inroads made by the sea along this stretch of coast, which continues to this day. But the problem has been shared across the generations – similar falls were recorded in 1799, 1825, 1852 and 1866, the latter costing the old lighthouse tower.

One of the aftermaths of the 1953 inundation was a need to improve coastal defences around the vulnerable North Norfolk coast. In this 1955 picture, workers prepare a revetment at Bacton, to be later secured by 16ft piling.

Microchips replaced humans as sentinels of the sea at Cromer Lighthouse in 1990 when Graham Fearn stepped down as the last lighthouse keeper. But the vital role of the lighthouse continues to this day, sending its beam out more than 20 miles into the North Sea. The EDP took this fascinating series of pictures in November 1952 to accompany an article about the vital, but sometimes lonely, role of the lighthouse team.

Principal keeper Mr J W Smith in the Watch Room keeps up the log, which recorded changing weather patterns and any unusual incidents during every 24-hour period. Mr Smith had spent 42 years in the service when this picture was taken, the fourth generation of his family to be a lighthouse keeper.

Much time was spent on polishing the 14 silver-lined 21-inch reflectors, and assistant keeper Mr C H Cherrett is pictured at the daily task. Cromer lighthouse was unique in Britain at the time in still having the last of the reflector-type optics, which in design went back to the oil-burning lighthouse days of the previous century.

Mr Smith again, this time changing one of the huge valves in the automatic radio beacon which was used to send out Morse signals twice every half hour in clear weather and every six minutes in fog.

(Left) Off duty, and the third keeper in the team, ex-Royal Navy man Martin Biddle is seen relaxing in his home at the foot of the tower. Watching Mr Biddle with his stamp collection was his wife, Joan.

(Bottom) This exterior view of the lighthouse was taken on April 6th 1956 and shows the 120-year-old lantern house a couple of years before its demolition and replacement by a modern light.

An historic moment took place at 1.30am on Monday August 28th 1967 when one of the largest gas pipelines in the world was brought ashore at Bacton. The last 1600 feet of the 34-mile pipeline had been laid in just over 11 hours, watched by hundreds of spectators. Here, a few hours before that milestone, workers bring the pipeline ever closer to the shore.

  The sea was about to yield up its riches once more – but this time its underground treasure.

Chapter Six

Fun, fun, fun

(Above) Melton Constable spring fair in May 1969 turned out to be an event with plenty of bounce, as this youngster discovered. The fair was to raise money for a minibus for use by the local youth club and secondary modern school.

(Right) Blooming lovely: Floral displays at the Aylsham Methodist Church flower festival being admired in April 1966.

Anglia presenter Bob Wellings (later a familiar face to millions of viewers through BBC's Nationwide) made the presentations after the 1968 Sheringham pancake race. Barbara Croxton, of Cromer Road, Holt, was the winner. Second in the Sheringham Chamber of Trade-organised contest was Annie Scarfe of Lower Bodham, who narrowly beat Jennifer Grand, of Cromer Road, Sheringham. Mr Wellings is seen presenting Barbara with her prize, a 50s shopping voucher – plus the inevitable frying pan!

Taking the strain: One of the tug-o'-war teams competing in the Holt Gala Day in town's community centre, and attractions included a procession of 25 floats.

August 1969. The gala was the third such event to be held to raise funds for the

(Left) Ahoy there: Some of the contestants in the fancy dress section of the fete to launch North Walsham Battle of Britain Week in September 1969. The fete, which was a success despite the typical late-summer showers, was opened by Miss Roz Early of Anglia TV.

(Below) Looking for bargains at the Walsingham WI fete on June 18th 1965.

They're off: The donkey derby gets under way at the North Norfolk Conservative fete at Barningham Hall, the home of Windsor MP Sir Charles Mott-Radclyffe. Our picture was taken in late July 1966.

An astonishing 40,000 people crammed into Thursford in September 1967 for the latest of George Cushing's "Bysteam" spectaculars. A 30-acre field had been set aside for the estimated 10,000 cars – but even that wasn't big enough. Mr Cushing's world-famous collection was heavily featured among the 120 exhibits.

Quick march: Townspeople enjoy some useful vantage points as majorettes get into their swing during the 1966 Sheringham Carnival.

Television personality Norman Vaughan was on hand at the Sheringham
Carnival on August 5th 1965 to crown its queen, Lynette Bowen, 18, plus her
attendants Janet Bell and Wendy Lewis. The carnival, which fielded 50 floats,
took place in almost perfect weather.

Children enjoy the fun at the August 1965 Wells Carnival. The event proved a success, despite summer showers.

(Opposite page, bottom) There was not a soapbox in sight at the Holt Carnival soapbox derby in the market place in July 1971 – but there were plenty of bits of bikes, prams and lawn mowers...

(Right) Miss RAFA North Walsham – Jean Larkin – congratulates four-year-old Debbie Brown after she had won first prize as a flower in the children's fancy dress section at the town's September 1967 Battle of Britain Carnival.

(Overleaf) Careful now...: Cromer Waiters' and Waitresses' Races are two of the fun events which make Cromer Carnival Week such a huge magnet for the crowds. The event, designed to test steady hands and speed, is run – or walked – on a course from the pier to the Bath House Hotel. In the 1969 race pictured dapper Cliff House Hotel entrant Vernon Sayka went for style rather than speed pace and was awarded the best-dressed waiter prize. The race itself was won by Louis Calderon (Hotel de Paris) and the waitresses' by Jenny Polydorou.

Chapter Seven

On the Town

The widely-acclaimed plan to refurbish Magdalen Street in Norwich drew admiration from towns around Norfolk – and a determination to emulate it. But few actually knuckled down to organising anything. Holt was the exception. "(The town) has gone about it with brisk efficiency," reported the EDP. Thirty-five properties were completely redecorated and another dozen partly refurbished in a campaign to brighten up the town centre. Our picture, taken on August 6th 1960, shows some of the spruced-up shops.

Shoppers bustle along Norwich Street, Fakenham, on a bright April 1st morning in 1965.

They were the days before bypasses when all traffic piled through North Walsham town centre – but you'd be hard-pressed to realise it, judging from the easy-going stance of the old timers doing a spot of mardling under the distinctive market cross in this shot, probably taken in the late 1940s or early 1950s.

97

Cromer's magnificent church tower dominates this lovely view of the town taken on September 9th 1956.

A tale of two Regals: The Regal Cinema at North Walsham was the town's second cinema (the original Picturedrome in King's Arms Street was built in 1912), and was opened on Monday September 7th 1931 by Guy Fanshawe, prospective Conservative candidate for East Norfolk. The capacity

audience enjoyed a programme which included British Movietone News and the main feature – Leslie Henson in A Warm Corner. But social changes such as the popularity of commercial television meant that the cinema could not see out the 1970s. It's hard to believe it now in this open-all-hours society that a move to open the cinema on Sundays provoked a vigorous pro- and anti-campaign, ending in a 1955 poll when 1075 voted in favour and 617 against. This August 20th 1970 picture shows the main attraction was the Clint Eastwood thriller Where Eagles Dare. The cinema is now a machine hire shop.

The Regal Cinema at Wells (right) closed for business on March 31st 1973, the same day as its sister cinema at Watton. Plans for Wells Town Council to use the building as a community hall fell through in 1977.

Cheers! Mark Wathen, local director of Barclays Bank, with the traditional pint at the topping-out ceremony at the firm's Aylsham site in February 1967. Barclays, in the town since the early 1800s, kept the original facade of the building, which was listed.

Two shoppers exchange a greeting on a rainy late November day in Sheringham in 1965.

"You can get anything you need in Cromer," said local traders on the eve of the town's trades fair in November 1960, when this picture was taken. And the bustling street scene tends to bear them out. Local shops in the picture include The Garden Shop, Gibson Bros, International Stores, Bryant and Utting, K Hardware and C Munday and Co.

Here's a picture to revive memories of anyone who grew up in the 1960s. An Aylsham shop (unidentified in the paper – but was it Granville Bonds, we wonder?) is stocking toys ready for the 1966 Christmas festivities. A Batman outfit and something called a "banshee screamer" were popular buys at 19s 11d (99p).

December 21st 1967, and the Christmas decorations in Fakenham Market Place are much in evidence over Saunders outfitters, to the left of the Crown.

The once-grand Marlborough Hotel at Cromer was in a sorry state of repair when this July 1955 picture was taken. A decision had been made to demolish about three-quarters of the landmark building, leaving the ballroom fronting Prince of Wales Road and the floors above it, plus the servery. When contractors moved in the following month the familiar cupola was the first to go. The site is now a garage. The hotel was one of many in the town to be demolished or turned into flats after the war, including the Royal Links, New Haven Court, Seaview and the Parry.

One little boy is unable to resist a peek at the camera in this October 1962 view of the heart of North Walsham.

A moment of calm at the Garden of Remembrance in North Walsham on
August 29th 1955.

Aylsham
Market Place,
pictured in
November
1968.

A flint's-eye-view of the eastern part of Cromer seafront shows an artist hard at work capturing the timeless beauty of the Cromer fishing boats. Recognisable vessels in this June 11th 1962 picture include the Miss Cromer (owned by Sidney Harrison) William Robert (Dennis Gaff), Autumn Rose (Jack Davies), Lewis James (Lewis Harrison) and My Beauty (Dick Davies).

(Overleaf) Woolworths had been looking for a large site in Fakenham for several years before they settled on the former Sheringham and Overman wool and seed merchants in Market Square. This picture was taken in the early 1960s while planners debated the Woolworths plan.

Chapter Eight

Faces and Places

Norfolk County Council learned to rue the day in 1969 it decided to order the enormously respected Sheringham fishmonger and lifeboatman Henry "Downtide" West to take down the sign that had been outside his High Street shop since 1913. Uproar ensued, and more than 3000 townspeople put their names to a petition to have the decision overthrown. A barrister – George Carman, no less – fought the case for Downtide at a planning inquiry held at St Peter's Parish Hall in front of a full and vocal Shannock audience. The county planning officer was regaled with jeers and cries of "Get yew back to Norwich!". Mr Carman summed up the issue with the memorable words: "If you think of Buckingham Palace you think of the Queen. When people think of this sign they think of Henry West." And the sign? It stayed put.

A dismantled old farm cart, perhaps? In fact the contraption pictured was the former Northrepps village fire engine. It was being prepared by John Golden (left) and Geoffrey Dixon for a bygones exhibition in August 1971.

Singer – now actor – Mark Wynter (remember his top five hit Venus in Blue Jeans?) provided a celebrity start to the Sidestrand Hall School fete in July 1969. Mark, who was appearing in a summer season show with Dora Bryan at Great Yarmouth, popped along the coast to help the special school and its efforts to raise money for a swimming pool. The event raised a very handsome £200 – and gave a lot of youngsters a chance to meet the singing star.

April 15th 1953, and on the left of our picture Brig D V Phelps and his bride-to-be the Hon Rosemary Cozens-Hardy – daughter of Lord and Lady Cozens-Hardy – are examining some of their gifts they had received at a party held for villagers at Letheringsett Hall.

This brightly-decorated gipsy caravan attracted the attention of many a traveller through Saxthorpe in August 1968. Villager Arthur Kidd – seen here with his son Joe and daughters Richenda (left) and Teresa – had bought the wagon. Mr Kidd estimated the van, known as a "dartboard wagon", was more than 150 years old.

Milkman Stanley Scott finally called it a day in April 1966 after delivering the milk to North Walsham for more than 40 years. He began in the milk trade, aged 14, working for Leonard Watts, and bought his own round for £15 a few years later. But even at 14 Stanley was no stranger to hard work. The 13th in a family of 14, he used to spend his weekends from the age of 11 helping his wherryman father David. That meant catching the 4.20pm train to Great Yarmouth on a Friday afternoon, loading the boat, then helping sail it to Wayford Bridge, where he was picked up by one of his brothers ready to go to school the next day. As if decades of getting up at 4.30am were not enough, Stanley also found time to be a retained fireman.

Hundreds of North Walsham mothers have cause to thank Mrs W A Belson, district nurse and midwife in the town for 33 years. Some of them are pictured at the party to mark Mrs Belson's retirement in September 1967.

Tarby's in town: Liverpudlian comic Jimmy Tarbuck was in Wells on June 14th 1968 to perform the official opening duties at the factory of handbag manufacturers D Maclaren. A popular attraction too, if the queue of autograph hunters is anything to go by.

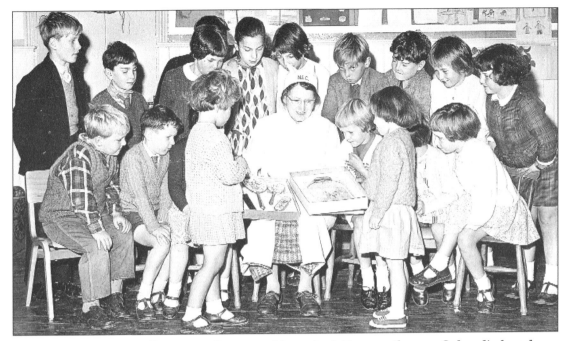

Never absent, never late was the proud boast of Baconsthorpe School's head cook Eva Bumphrey who is surrounded by some of the school's pupils on her retirement in October 1965 in this charming study. Pupils Andrea Smith and Thomas Worboys made the retirement presentations.

Cheers!: Aylsham group Barry Lee and the Planets – and their Hunstanton manager – celebrate turning professional on October 8th 1965. The group, formed in 1962, consisted of Barry, 19; Tony Dyball, 20; Angus Jarvis, 20; Roger Reynolds, 19, and Mike Dyball. Mike, Tony and Roger later turned themselves into the famous Brother Lees comedy group.

"I've had a fantastically interesting life," claimed Aylsham businesswoman Clare Hoare in a 1989 profile. The founder of the famous Black Sheep woollens company came to Norfolk in 1955 with husband Gerard, but it was not until 1966 that an incident happened which changed her life. Her mower broke down – so she sold it and bought some black Welsh mountain sheep instead. Mrs Hoare has also found time to be a qualified pilot, tennis coach and Foreign Office registrar. Oh, and she's Richard Branson's aunt too....

The Royal Observer Corps, which was founded in 1925 to combat the growing threat from aerial bombardment, was disbanded in the post-Cold War world of the early 1990s. But between those dates thousands of men and women had performed sterling service in providing observation services of the skies in war and peace. This November 1969 picture shows an open day held by the Aylsham corps, a member of Number 6 Norwich Group. Pictured at the event, held at Aylsham Primary School, were, from left, observer officer C Williamson, observer A Roberts, leading observer E Gant, observer officer C J Taylor, observer D W March and chief observer J E Wymer. The piece of equipment they were inspecting was, chillingly, a device for detecting the position of a nuclear bomb blast.

"And the producer said...": Comedian Ronnie Corbett was returning a favour to Cromer when he came to open the secondary modern school's teaching pool on June 25th 1971. For audiences in the town helped give him an early break in his career when he appeared in Out of the Blue at the Parish Hall in the 1950s.

Chapter Nine

At Play

(Above) Wheel good: Sheringham Urban District Council chairman Mr H J Child presents cycling proficiency certificates to 30 pupils of the town's primary school in May 1966. Mr Child was accompanied by PC Colin Higson.

(Right) It's mine: Cheryl Hensby gives a special hug to her prize bear at the Aylsham Primary School's Teddy Bears' Picnic in July 1971. Looking on in envy are Serena Newstead, Sharon Toner, Nicola Howlett and Wendy Thurnby.

At the pines at Wells beach in August 1961, the holidaymakers are taking it easy – simply soaking up the sun...

...while over the other side of the pines, on the same day, the boating lake at Abraham's Bosom proves a more active attraction.

(Overleaf) Proud moment: Fakenham Town Band pose in their new uniforms at the Eastern Counties Newspapers annual garden party at the Bixley Manor home of Timothy (now Sir Timothy) and Lady Mary Colman on June 23rd 1967.

(Above) West Runton Scouts seen in action during the trek cart challenge at the Norfolk Youth Service presentation day at the Holt Hall centre on July 8th 1967.

(Right) In harmony: North Walsham Girl Guides prepare for a televised family service at St George's Church in April 1971.

All together now: Some of the many young people who took part in the Sheringham and district Schools Music Festival in June 1969 go through their paces.

Miles of smiles: Fakenham Scouts are pictured collecting a "Wensum Mile of Pennies" in the town's market place for their funds as part of a week of events in May 1970.

Cooling off: Making a splash at Goggs Mill at Hempton on the outskirts of Fakenham in August 1953.

Cockles are a popular North Norfolk dish. Here two 1950s holidaymakers are gathering the fruits of their labours on Wells beach.

Little Snoring Airfield opened in July 1943 and became part of Bomber Command's offensive on Germany. But by the time this October 1960 picture was taken, members of the Tiger Flying Club had taken over where Lancasters, Mosquitoes, Defiants and Beaufighters had once flown. Plaques in the village church of St Andrew record the heroism of the wartime airmen.

River Buoy, ridden by owner Major E W O T Wilson, holds off the challenge of Treasurer to win the Queen's Cup at the West Norfolk Hunt Steeplechase meeting on April 11th 1955. Inspired by the exciting finish, the EDP claimed "This was one of the best races ever seen at Fakenham."

It was still known as Whit Monday in those days, and the crowds on May 21st 1956 did what generations of people have done before and since on bank holidays – head for the coast. Temperatures reached 60 degrees Fahrenheit around Cromer (where our picture was taken) and Sheringham. But Wells was not so lucky, with the beach affected by, in the words of the EDP, a "not very enticing" north-easterly wind. Was there a touch of tongue in cheek about the paper's report summing up the day? "Cafes did a brisk trade... and hoteliers appeared to be satisfied."

Aldborough fair is one of the all-too-few village fairs still continuing – and what an stretches back almost 800 years to the reign of King John. By the 18th century fair for country folk as the years passed. The fair was traditionally started by the 1964.

evocative history it has. Traditionally held on the longest days of the year, its story
the event was a major meeting place for the gentry, although it became an ordinary
oldest villagers playing "tipcat". Our picture was taken on the evening of June 20th

Concentration: Keen interest in the rushwork class at Beeston Regis WI in this 1950s picture.

We don't have a date for this picture of a Fakenham Telephone Exchange open day, but we would put it sometime in the 1950s. The Queen's Road exchange was manned 24 hours a day, seven days a week from February 2nd 1944 until its closure in February 1983 – by then it was the smallest of its type left in the country. One amusing EDP story from the archives tells of extra lunchtime staff being put on from October 1957. The reason? A flood of calls to local bookmakers before the start of the 2pm races!

Rosemary Callaby with Duke and Gypsy during the horse ploughing contest at Holt Farmers' Club's annual ploughing match at Hempstead in October 1967.

The North Norfolk Harriers prepare to set off from Cromer Hall on January 5th 1962. Master of the Hunt Major J Barclay is on the right of the picture.

The magnificent Long Gallery of Blickling Hall was the appropriate setting for thi

June 24th 1961 performance of Elizabethan music by the Julian Bream Consort.

Making our own entertainment: July 20th 1955 saw a remarkable display of self-help by holidaymakers and local people at Cromer. In an attempt to re-make the horseshoe pool on the west beach – which provided safer bathing closer to the shore – organisers asked volunteers to help shift the tons of rock needed. In the event several thousand people turned out to help, with special coach parties even coming from Great Yarmouth. Men from HMS Pincher enlivened proceedings by holding "King Neptune's Court" all afternoon. Curiously, the "sentences" all seemed to be one thing – hard labour moving rocks!

The Norfolk County branch library at Holt Road, Fakenham, proved a hit with borrowers when it opened for business in April 1951. Under the watchful eye of Librarian Miss J C Houlder, the library opened three days a week. This picture was taken on May 6th 1953 to highlight the library's success at attracting more than 650 young members.

Chapter Ten

Animal Magic

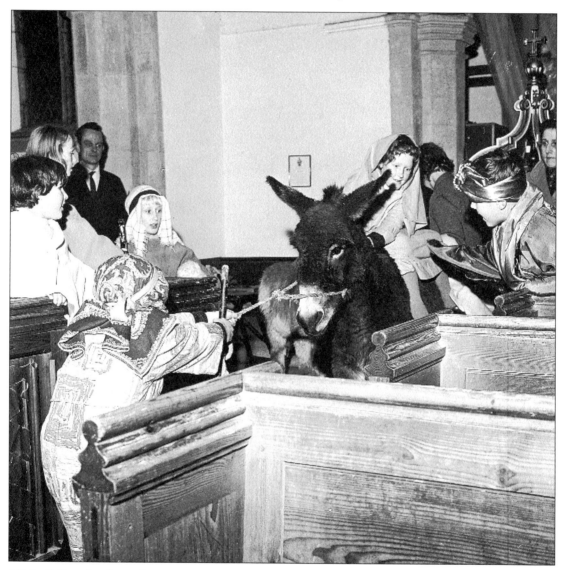

Mabel the donkey decided that being led up the aisle for Runton Sunday School's Nativity play on December 17th 1969 was just not for her. So she stayed put and refused to budge. Refused, that is, until some judicious pushing and pulling – and the offer of a juicy carrot – led to a change of heart. Just as well the display of donkey temperament was at the dress rehearsal and not the performance itself.

Altogether more well behaved, Bilco the donkey played a part in the Nativity staged at St Botolph's Church, Banningham, in December 1966. Parts were played by local children including Helen Seaman, James Keeler, Andrew Keeler, Hazel Allaway, Rebecca Hall, Jennifer Walker, Jacqueline Allaway, Carol Watson, April Seaman, Margaret Hall, Stephen Hall, Joanna van Poortvliet, Diana Allaway, Katherine Muirhead and Heather Hall.

Ten-year-old Harry Wright found himself acting as a surrogate mother when one of his father's ewes gave birth to quins in February 1966. To help the mother cope with the four surviving lambs, Harry hand-fed them with a mixture of cow's milk and glucose.

Two pictures from May 1967: (Above) Dillow de Bedous, a white Pyrenean mountain dog, hogged the limelight when the EDP visited Sheringham and District Kennel Association Show. Cheryl and Brent Webster are also pictured. (Right) Mrs Hubert Blount of Cley Old Hall measures her six-day-old Shetland colt. The foal was just 21 inches tall, compared with its 32-inch mother.

April 1967, and the EDP cameras captured this timeless picture of Paul Kidd of Briston with a horse and foal.

A tricky judging job for RSPCA Ch Insp C G Marshall at the April 1966 Northrepps School pet show. Watching him are David Ward and Julie Stevenson. The eventual winner was Gillian Smith's dog Patsy.

This chestnut horse peering over its field gate caught the eye of an EDP photographer travelling through Hunworth on April 30th 1974.

Rebecca, a three-year-old ewe, was an unusual sight in the lanes around Upper Sheringham around 1970. The ewe, seen here with her owner Helen Clarke, lived a pampered life at The Lodge. Miss Clarke nursed Rebecca when a sickly lamb and soon had her frisking about. The lucky animal had a most unsheeplike favourite meal: fish and chips!

Mary had a little lamb: A special day for the youngsters at Fakenham Play
School in March 1971 when one of the more cuddly products of spring was
shown to the class.